Written and Illustrated by Caroline Arnold

# A Day and Night in the RAIN FOREST

PICTURE WINDOW BOOKS
a capstone imprint

*Cricka, cricka!* call the toucans.
Time to wake up!

It is early morning in the Amazon rain forest.
The noisy birds hop from branch to branch,
looking for food. They find ripe fruit and
pick it with their long bills.

A toucan's call can be heard up to a half mile
(0.8 kilometers) away. Howler monkeys can be
heard as far away as 3 miles (4.8 km).

The eerie calls of a troop of howler monkeys fill the air. These large monkeys are looking for food too. They swing through the trees, holding on with their hands, feet, and tails. They find fresh leaves and settle down to eat.

3

An iguana sits in a patch of sunlight and warms its scaly body. Its spiny back warns other animals to stay away. Then, gripping branches with its long claws, the iguana searches for flowers, fruit, and leaves to eat.

A snake's jaws can separate, allowing it to swallow food larger than the width of its body.

Nearby, an emerald tree boa hangs from a branch. It hides among the green leaves. The snake waits for a bird or small animal to come close. Quick as a wink, it snatches its prey in its wide jaws and swallows it whole.

5

Coatis scamper along the shady forest floor. They snort, scream, and whistle to one another. They look for leaves, fruit, and nuts up in the trees and on the ground. Coatis will eat almost anything, including insects and dead animals. But they stay away from the colorful poison frogs!

More than 1,000 kinds of frogs live in the Amazon rain forest. They catch insects with their long tongues. The tiny poison frogs are active only during the day. Their skin is poisonous. The frogs' bright colors warn predators not to eat them.

Coatis are related to raccoons. They use their long tails for balance as they climb.

The air feels thick and sticky. Clouds gather, and rain falls. High in the trees, a sleeping sloth hangs from a branch. When the rain stops, the sloth opens its eyes. It slowly reaches for a leaf. It slowly munches the leaf. Then it curls up and goes to sleep again.

Sloths do everything slowly. Their slow movements make it harder for predators to spot them. Sloths are the main food for harpy eagles. When an eagle finds a sloth, it grabs it with its powerful talons.

Harpy eagles are among the largest birds in the world. Their talons are more than 5 inches (13 centimeters) long!

Shadows grow long. Daytime animals look for safe places to spend the night. Nighttime animals wake up.

A giant armadillo comes out of its burrow. It finds a termite mound and digs into it with its strong feet and claws. The termites scurry, but the armadillo catches them with its long, sticky tongue.

Nearby, an ocelot yawns and stretches its legs. It listens for the sounds of small animals. All night long it will prowl the forest looking for prey.

The ocelot's eyes contain a layer called the tapetum. It reflects light and helps the ocelot see in the dark.

11

Bats find their way in the dark by listening to the echoes of their own sounds. This is called echolocation.

The moon rises over the tops of the trees. Bats flap their wings and take off into the cool night. Some swoop after insects. Others look for flowers and fruit. Vampire bats search for blood.

Owl monkeys climb among the high branches.
Their large eyes help them see in the dark.
They search for flowers, fruit, insects, and
leaves. A moth flies by, and a monkey snatches
and eats it.

13

On the damp forest floor, a tarantula comes out of its burrow. Tapirs grab twigs, shoots, fruits, and berries with their long snouts. Deer nibble leaves among the bushes. As the deer and tapirs search for food, they watch and listen for hungry jaguars.

Tarantulas are the biggest spiders in the world. Some have bodies more than 3 inches (8 cm) long and legs up to 5 inches (13 cm).